The Creator's

Devon Rex
CATS

by C. S. Ellicott

Sweetwater Still Publishing, Oklahoma, USA

ISBN: 978-1-7356345-3-1
LCCN: 2021944292

Published by Sweetwater Hollow Homeschool, an imprint of Sweetwater Still Publishing -- 56893 S. 695 Rd., Colcord OK
Printed in the United States of America
26 25 24 23 22 21 / 12 11 10 9 8 7 6 5 4 3

For my grandchildren:

The LORD's love is
with those who fear him,
and his righteousness
with their grandchildren.

Psalm 103:17

The Story of Kirlee

"Whatever is good and perfect is a gift to us from God our Father, who created all the lights in the heavens."
James 1:17

It was a dark, rainy summer night in England. The year was 1959. Near a village in the county of Devon, a stray cat raced past the tin mine and over the hills. The clouds poured down rain. Thunder rumbled and arrows of lightning flashed. The little cat was homeless, but she knew where to get out of the rain, and where to find food and kindness. So she ran until she came to a small house. She scrambled onto the back porch and out of the rain. She stood at the door and cried:

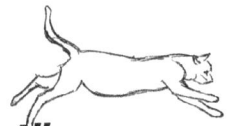

"Mew! Meow! Meeeowwww!"

3

Soon a lady came out with a cup and saucer in her hands. "Well hello!" the lady said. "Hungry, are you? Here it is!"

The lady, named Miss Cox, set the cup of milk in front of the cat. Then she set down the full saucer of food and stepped back so the cat would not be afraid. The thin cat tiptoed up to the bowl and began to take large bites, stopping often to look around. Miss Cox did not try to pet the shy cat.

"Alright then?" Miss Cox asked. "Oh, but look at your belly!" she said. Indeed, the cat's middle looked huge on her very thin body. "Going to be a mother, are you?" she asked.

Miss Cox went back into her home. Moments later she came back with a box. Inside the box was a soft blanket. "Here my dear," she said. "You'll need this soon!" The little cat watched Miss Cox put the box into a dark, dry corner. The cat took the last bite of her food and then drank some milk. Then she crept slowly to the corner and sniffed the box. After a pause, she climbed in and laid down.

Love is a safe, warm place!

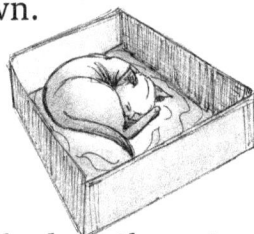

The next time Miss Cox checked on the cat, she had a lovely litter of kittens. Each day Miss Cox set out milk and food for the hungry mother cat. Since this was a safe, friendly place—with food and drink— the mother cat stayed and kept her kittens there.

When the kittens were two weeks old, their eyes were open and they began to look around.

A few weeks later they were scampering around the yard. At this time, Miss Cox saw that one kitten did not look like the others. He was a rather odd looking curly-haired kitten! Miss Cox had never seen a kitten with curly hair. She decided to keep him, and she named him Kirlee.

A Different Sort of Kitten

In the 1950s there were almost no curly cats. So why was Kirlee curly?

Kirlee's fur was caused by a *gene* that *mutated*. A *gene* is kind of like a building block with a recipe on it. *Mutate* means to change. So a *mutated gene* is a gene that suddenly changed the recipe!

Kirlee had many genes. All bodies have genes. Your body has many genes. A cat's body has many genes. The recipe written in genes is called a *code*. The code in a cat's genes says THIS WILL BE A CAT! The code also says what color the cat's fur will be. Genes say how big the cat's body will be. They say what shape its eyes will be, and many other things.

Genes are *inherited*. That means Kirlee's genes came from both his mother and from his father.

Kirlee's father was a big, black stray cat who lived at the tin mine. The big cat had long hair, and his tail was covered in curls!

Kirlee's father had a *mutated gene*—also called a *genetic mutation*. The *mutated gene* gave him curls on his tail. But when Kirlee was born, he was the only kitten who got the *mutation*. The *mutation* changed more than just Kirlee's fur. It changed Kirlee's body in many ways!

Kirlee was more muscular. He could climb better. He had long, thin legs, and longer back legs than most cats. He also had a very odd head shape, like a wedge or a piece of pie. He had high cheek bones, a flat skull, a short nose, extra big eyes, and very large ears!

But Kirlee's brothers and sisters did not seem to care how odd he looked. And his mother loved them all the same.

Kirlee was a very happy kitten.

Science Moment

gene *(jeen) noun, plural* genes. One of the very tiny parts of matter found in all animal and plant cells, serving to determine which characteristics are passed on to its offspring.

mutate *(mew tayt) verb.* To change and cause an unusual characteristic to develop in a plant or animal; to change into something very different.

mutation *(mew tay shun) noun.* A sudden, abnormal change or alteration in a genetically determined structure.

code *(koud) noun.* A set of words, signs, or symbols used to send messages or give information; a set of laws or regulations.

inherit *(in hair it) verb.* To receive (something) from someone who had it previously; to have (a characteristic, disease, etc.) because of the genes that you get from your parents when you are born.

nature *(nay cher) noun.* Basic character and qualities of a person or thing; genetically controlled qualities.

Normal cat

Kirlee

Kirlee Meets the World!

Kirlee was a very playful kitten. He loved his owner, Miss Cox, and she loved him. He followed her around just like a puppy. In fact, he even liked to play fetch! Miss Cox said Kirlee acted more like a puppy than a cat! He also climbed like a little monkey. And Kirlee had extra long toes that he used to hold things. He was very different!

While Kirlee was still little, Miss Cox read in the newspaper that there would be a cat show soon. The article said that "the only curly kitten in Britain" was going to be at the show. Next to the article there was a picture of a curly kitten named Du-Bu Lambtex.

"Aha!" laughed Miss Cox. "Du-Bu Lambtex is *not* the only curly kitten in the country!" she said. Right away Miss Cox sat down and wrote a letter to the owner of Du-Bu Lambtex. "I have a curly kitten too!" she wrote. And that was how the world found out about Kirlee!

Miss Cox and her good friend Miss Croll took Kirlee to the cat show. Kirlee met many people and many cats! Miss Cox and her friend found out that Kirlee was not related to the other curly cats in the world. Kirlee had a brand new *mutation!*

Now other people wanted cats like Kirlee. But they could not find any. Yes, Kirlee's father had curls, and now and then a curly kitten would be seen. But the countryside did not have a whole bunch of curly cats running free.

Genetic mutations are often weak and fragile. *Mutations* need lots of care, like plants in a garden. If *genetic mutations* are not preserved, they can die out. So Miss Cox and her friends agreed to work hard to preserve this *genetic mutation.* They would let Kirlee have many closely related kittens. This way the *gene* that gave him his curls would not be lost.

When Kirlee grew up, he was the father of many kittens. When Kirlee grew old there were lots of his curly grandchildren and great grandchildren in the world.

Kirlee's Curls Tell a Story

"Through everything God made,
people can clearly see his invisible qualities—
his eternal power and divine nature.
So they have no excuse for not knowing God."
Romans 1:20

The Bible says that we can learn about God by looking at what He created. And we can learn a lot from *mutated genes!* Even though people loved Kirlee's curls and his odd shape, *mutations* are not really a good thing. They are almost always bad and harmful. They cause weakness.

Kirlee's father had a *mutation* that changed his fur, so he did not have *normal cat fur*. But did you know that all of the cats in the world came from *just two cats?!*

God created all things in just six days. On the last day of creation, God made cats. And he made them able to have babies that would be just like them.

Then **God said, "Let us make people in our image, to be like us."** But who was God talking to? Who helped God make cats and people? When God said "like us," He was talking to Himself! The Bible shows us that there is only one God. But he has three parts: God the Father, God the Son, and God the Holy Spirit.

So when God created the first cats and the first people, he worked "together" with Himself. And He talked to *Himself* about it. He wanted the people to be different from the animals. He created humans "in his own image," to be like Him. He created one man (named Adam) and one woman (named Eve.) Then God blessed them and told them to rule over everything. They were to rule over the fish in the sea, the birds in the sky, and all the animals that scurried along the ground.

God let Adam give names to all of the animals. Adam even named the little furry animals that purred. Do you know what he named them?

Then on the seventh day God rested from all of His work. He blessed the seventh day and called it *holy*.

God put Adam and Eve in the Garden of Eden. And they took a walk with God every day. Do you think the cats followed them on their walk?

Living in the Garden and walking with God was a very good life. **But then something very bad and terrible happened . . .**

Creation Begins to Mutate!

Things were going so well! The people had a great place to live. They had God's breath (His Spirit) in their hearts! God took walks with them in the cool of the day. And they had really cute cats!

God did not create the world full of pain or death. There was a tree in the garden called the "Tree of Life." The people ate from it and they never grew old. Nothing ever died. People and animals lived happily with God.

But they had one rule they had to obey. God gave them a garden filled with trees. They could eat from almost all of the trees. But in the middle of the lovely garden there was one tree they were not allowed to eat from. "If you eat its fruit, you will be doomed to die," God said.

God had an enemy named Satan. He used to be one of God's angels. But he was proud and he rebelled against God. Then he was thrown out of heaven.

Now Satan was jealous of Adam and Eve. He wanted to trick them and make them disobey God. If the people broke God's laws, the world would be cursed! Yes, even the cats would suffer.

People were made *in God's image*. God is perfect and He never disobeys or does evil. So if the people disobeyed, they would not be like God anymore! They would break the mold (image) they were created in, and a curse would fall on all creation.

"God created humans in his own image.
In the image of God he created them;
male and female he created them."
Genesis 1:27

One day Satan entered the garden as a snake. He asked Eve, "Did God really say you must not eat the fruit from any of the trees in the garden?"

Eve answered, "We can eat fruit from the trees in the garden. It's only the fruit from the tree in the middle of the garden that we are not allowed to eat. God told us, 'You must not eat it or even touch it; if you do, you will die.'"

"You won't die!" the snake said, lying. Satan wanted Eve to think God had lied. "God knows that your eyes will be opened as soon as you eat it, and you will be like God, knowing both good and evil," the snake said.

Eve listened to him and she was tricked. The tree was pretty. Its fruit looked tasty. And Eve wanted wisdom. So she took some of the fruit and ate it. Then she gave some to her husband, Adam. He ate it too.*

Suddenly their eyes were opened. They felt very ashamed, and a curse fell on the whole world.

* GENESIS 3

Mutations Tell the Future

"Against its will, all creation was subjected to God's curse."
Romans 8:20

Adam and his wife Eve were banished from the beautiful Garden. They were cursed, and the world was cursed with them. Even the cats suffered.

Do you think the cats had to leave the garden too? I think they did. Everything changed. The animals still had babies that were *almost* like them. But they were not perfect anymore. Things began to *mutate* and to grow old and die.

People had babies too. But humans were not quite like God anymore. Children *inherited* a *sinful nature*—like a *gene* that made them feel like disobeying. This *sin gene* made people feel selfish. They began to lie and steal. They began to get angry and hurt each other. They began to feel sad.

A *mutation* is almost always bad. *Mutations* make our bodies weaker. Most *mutations* are just a little harmful, but others are very harmful. Most of these bad *mutations* pass on to the next generation, so each generation is more *mutant*. As time goes by, the bodies of people and animals become weaker because they have more *mutations*. The world is a "corrupted creation." It is not good like God created it to be.

Mutations in our body's codes (and in the codes of our cats) tell us that we live on a young earth. Scientists used to think the earth was millions of years old. Some still think that, but their belief is not based on new studies.

Scientists used to say that if the *mutation* rate were "as high as one per generation" life would be destroyed in time. But now, with new technology and better tests, scientists know the rate is between 100 to 300 harmful *mutations* per person!*

Genetic codes *mutate* at rates much higher than they thought. Science has now proven that the world cannot be more than about 6000 years old. Earth cannot have been here for millions of years, or it would have already gone extinct.

Life that *mutates* this fast cannot last forever. In fact, many scientists believe that creation has a total expected life span of only about 6000 years.** This means the life of earth and its creatures is nearly over.

But before you start to worry, remember that God loves His creation. Sin and disobedience brought a curse, but God had a plan! God's plan would destroy the curse and bring the people back into a beautiful garden where they could walk with Him once again.

"But Jesus Christ has rescued us from the curse pronounced by the law. When he was hung on the cross, he took upon himself the curse for our wrongdoing."
Galatians 3:13

* Dr. John Sanford, *Genetic Entropy and the Mystery of the Genome*
** Dr. Everett McKibben, G.H McKibben, *As the Human Race is Degenerating* 20

Do Cats Go to Heaven?

". . . all creation looks forward to the day
when it will join God's children in glorious
freedom from death and decay."
Romans 8:21

Someday God's creation will be free from the curse caused by disobedience. The Bible doesn't say if cats go to heaven or not. But it says that all animals will be free from suffering and death.

Do you remember when God created the world? He spoke and the light appeared. He used His Words to create things, and He talked to Himself. There is only one God. But all three "persons" of God worked together. God the Father, God the Son, and the Holy Spirit created everything.

Do you remember that Satan became a snake so that he could hurt the people and animals? By his trick, the world was cursed. Sin and disobedience came into the world like a really bad *mutation*. Every person became guilty of sin and rebellion.

But God had a plan to defeat the curse and to forgive people for their sin. God is way more powerful than Satan.

When the time was right, God also came into the world. But God did not come as a sneaky snake to hurt people. God came as a perfect human named Jesus. Jesus is also called "the Word." He is the same "person" of God that spoke and created the world! The Word (Jesus) came into the world to save us. The Bible tells the story like this:

"...this is how God loved the world: He gave his one and only Son, so that everyone who believes in him will not perish but have eternal life. God sent his Son into the world not to judge the world, but to save the world through him."
John 3:16-17

Your Creator loves you! Jesus is called the Word, and Jesus is your Creator. He came to rescue you. He destroyed the curse and death.

If you trust Jesus to set you free from the curse, you can become God's child. And the third "person" of God—the Holy Spirit—will come to live in your heart.

Your sins can be forgiven. You can be a new person. The Spirit of Jesus living inside of you can give you the strength to break free from the power of the *sin gene!*

Pray this prayer:

Dear Jesus, please forgive me for the bad

things I have done. Set me free from the curse.

Put your Holy Spirit in my heart. Show me

how to walk with you. And bring me into the

garden in heaven some day.

Amen.

The Devon Rex Cat is Talking to You!

All creation speaks of God, so we have no excuse if we say we don't know about Him. But *mutant* cats tell us about Adam and Eve's disobedience. *Mutations* remind us that the world is cursed and it will not last forever. *Mutant* cats tell you that you need someone to save you!

There is only one way to be saved. There is only one way to God. There is only one way to heaven. Jesus is your Creator who came to earth to set you free from the curse. He wants you to know Him. He wants you to walk with Him.

God created the Devon Rex to help

you find your way to heaven!

The Story of Monkey the Cat

"The Lord is close to the brokenhearted;
he rescues those whose spirits are crushed."
Psalm 34:18

Monkey was a Devon Rex kitten who loved to climb, just like a monkey. He was a happy kitten. He lived with a family who loved him.

But Monkey was born with a very weak heart. The doctor said he would not live very long. This made his family sad. They hoped the doctor was wrong.

For awhile Monkey did not seem sick. He loved to run and jump and climb. He liked to sit on his people. He liked their shoulders best. And when they were busy, he would sit in his favorite chair.

But one day when he was almost grown up, he followed his favorite girl outside. She didn't see him behind her. Then she went back into the house.

Monkey had never been outside before. He had never been alone before. His heart began to beat faster and faster . . . He was very scared. So he hid himself.

℃

That night his family could not find him. They stayed up after dark looking for him. He heard them. But he was afraid of the dark and he was too afraid to move. So he kept hiding.

He was all alone. It was a terrible feeling. In fact, it felt so horrible that it hurt his weak heart.

Monkey's family looked for him for days. But he kept hiding. His heart felt so weak and broken that he could not run to them. He could not make a sound.

But finally, after three days, he took a deep breath and began to cry loudly: "MEOW!!!!! MEOW!!! MEOW!!! MEEEEEEEOOWWWWWWWWWWW!!!" he said.

His family heard his cries. They ran to save him.

ɞ

At last Monkey was safe in his bed again. But he had been so scared and alone. Now he got sick. He stayed in his bed most of the time. All of his hair fell out. He did not want to eat or drink.

Monkey was very sick for a long time. His family knew he had a weak heart. When he was lost, it was bad for his heart.

Now Monkey spent most of his time sleeping. He did not sit on his people. He did not visit his favorite chair. One day Monkey heard his family talking about him.

"My heart will break when he is gone," said his favorite girl.

"Let's pray and ask Jesus to help us," said her mother. Monkey heard them talking. Then he went back to sleep. Some time later, Monkey heard lots of noise. His family was laughing. He went back to sleep. But all of a sudden, he heard a new sound. It went like this:

"MEW! MEW! MEW!"

Monkey's eyes opened wide! He sat up. He stood up. He crawled from his bed. Monkey limped slowly to the front room. He saw his family playing with a small, white kitten!

The little kitten had lots of curls. His family smiled at the kitten. His favorite girl called to the kitten, "Come here, Casey!" The kitten ran to her and climbed into her lap. Monkey's favorite girl laughed and held the soft, curly kitten. They were sitting in Monkey's favorite chair.

No one saw Monkey standing there looking weak . . . and bald. Monkey was not happy.

That day Monkey did not go back to bed. He stayed up to watch his family play with Casey the kitten. He did not like this. He was the family cat. He did not want to share his family. In fact, he did not want to share anything!

When Casey saw him, she ran to him. She tried to cuddle with him. Monkey hissed at her and moved away.

Monkey jumped up on the couch.

The kitten followed him.

Monkey jumped down from the couch.

The kitten followed him.

CB

Monkey did not want Casey to have his family, so he never went to bed in the daytime again. He also ate all of his food. He didn't want the kitten to get it! He started drinking lots of water. And he grew some of his curls back! His family was amazed and happy. Monkey was not sick anymore! They thanked God for answering their prayers.

But they still played with the curly little kitten every day.

☙

Every day Monkey sat in his favorite chair, all by himself. When Casey tried to join him, he hissed at her. Day after day, Monkey sat all alone, growing his fur and hissing when she came close. He ate more food than ever before. And he drank more water. His body felt stronger, but he was not happy. He felt very sad and lonely.

☙

Monkey's family loved him. Casey the kitten showed him love too. But broken hearts don't heal that easy. Hearts cannot start to heal until the love gets inside of them and starts to grow! Hearts are not fully healed until we start letting the love pour out of us onto others.

CB

One day, Monkey was sitting in his favorite chair alone. Casey was bigger now. She knew he didn't want her in his chair, so she played on the floor near him. She was batting a soft ball back and forth. Monkey tried not to watch. But it looked like fun . . . and he was tired of feeling so alone.

After awhile the kitten picked up the little soft ball with her mouth. She scampered up to Monkey's chair and looked at him. Monkey looked away. But he did not hiss this time. So she jumped softly up onto the corner of the chair. She dropped her ball and it rolled close to Monkey. Monkey looked happy. Casey looked happy.

Then she moved closer to him. Monkey did not hiss or move away, so she laid down next to him. And then she started to purr.

At last, Monkey gave a great big sigh.

Then he started to purr too.

From that day on, Monkey shared everything with Casey. And Monkey lived for many happy years.

The End

Dear friends,
Love one another,
For love comes
From God.

www.ingramcontent.com/pod-product-compliance
Lightning Source LLC
Chambersburg PA
CBHW021123020426
42331CB00004B/599